How to Grow a Chair

The Art of Tree Trunk Topiary

By Richard Reames
and
Barbara Hahn Delbol

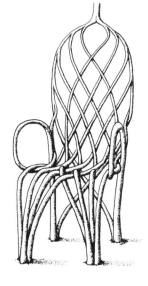

❖ ❖ ❖

Arborsmith Studios
Williams, Oregon

Distributed by Arborsmith Studios

Printed in the United States of America

Library of Congress Catalag No.: 95-094508

ISBN: 0-9647280-0-1

First printing August 1995

Table of Contents

Acknowledgments

Special thanks go to the many people who helped bring this book to publication. They include:

Photos: Covalo and Covalo Photography - Ed Webber's vintage photos of Axel Erlandson's Tree Circus
Cosme Castanieto Photography, Nevada City, Calif.
Pat Reames
Debbie Reames
Richard C. Reames
Barbara Delbol

Cover design: Gilliam Garcia, GMG Graphics

Illustrations: Adam Wick Sylvan - text illustrations
Bob Cremins - rear cover illustration

Printing: Greg Cornwell of Monument Litho and Prepress

Others:
Mark Primack, for graciously sharing information on Axel Erlandson
Wilma Erlandson, for insight into the life of her father
Kirk LeShell and Michael Bonafonte for access to Erlandson's surviving trees at Bonafonte's "Hecker Pass - A Family Adventure"
Arliss Reames for information retrieval
Dr. Alex L. Shigo for information on tree trunk topiary
Ray Prag, Cathy Escot, Ken Richards and Alison Aldrich for editing assistance
Buddha John for his brainstorming
Java House, Grants Pass, Ore., for its creative space
Maya Many Moons Reames for her creative inspiration and support

About the Authors

Richard Reames is a nursery owner, artist, author and father. He owns and operates Arborsmith Studios in Williams, Oregon, with his wife and daughter, and lives in an octogon log home he and his wife built from dead standing pine, cedars and Douglas fir. He was raised in the Santa Cruz mountains of California and attended Stanislaus State College in Turlock, Calif. He conceived and wrote the original manuscript for this book.

Barbara Hahn Delbol is a writer and editor with the Grants Pass Daily Courier in Grants Pass, Oregon. She and her husband also own and operate Althouse Nursery in Cave Junction, Oregon, which propagates and sells native plant seedlings for forest restoration projects. She edited and designed this book.

Forward

In this book, you will find an introduction to a new field of art using live, growing trees as the medium.

This art was pioneered by Axel Erlandson who demonstrated some of its possibilities by shaping more than 70 mature sculptures at his roadside attraction named The Tree Circus (1947-1963.)

Erlandson was secretive about how he shaped his trees and what he learned about the techniques. In writing this book, I wrestled with the thought of holding back some of my best ideas for use exclusively at my own nursery. But I finally concluded that we are in the "information age" and any attempt to constrict the flow of ideas will only lead to my own constriction.

Many fine books have been written on the subjects of trees, pruning, grafting and topiary. I've listed many of these in the *Resources* section at the end of this book. It is not the intent of this book to replace that vast body of information. These topics, though, are briefly covered as the relate to Arborsculpture.

May your trees grow strong, your grafts always take, and may the bluebird of happiness nest in your Arborsculptures.

Enjoy!

Richard Reames

This book is dedicated to the memory of
Axel Erlandson

CHAPTER ONE

From the very beginning, the lives of humans and trees have been woven together in the fabric of life. On a physical level, trees have provided food, shelter, fuel and medicine. In modern industrial times, trees have given us building materials, pulp and paper. Most importantly, science has shown that trees are instrumental in creating and maintaining our soil and climate - the earth and air so necessary for survival.

Trees in Religion

On a spiritual level, trees have played important roles in religion through all world cultures. For example, the Tree of Knowledge and the Tree of Life in the Garden of Eden are primary images in the Christian and Judaic religions.

In Buddhism, the Buddha obtains enlightenment while sitting under a pipal tree at Bodh Gaya while the Hindu god Vishnu is said to have been born under a banyan tree. The pipal tree, Ficus religiosa, is worshipped by the Buddhists of India. Also, each Buddha of India is associated with his own bodhi tree - the Buddhist equivalent of the Tree of Knowledge.[1]

In the Americas, the great Iroquois Confederacy comprised of five American Indian nations, had a sacred Peace Tree. In central

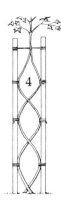

American lore, the Toltec ruler, Quetzalcoatl, formed a following of people called the "Fellowship of the Tree of Life" around a particular sacred tree growing in Oaxaca, Mexico. The Aztecs also planted a tree for every child who was born into their community.

More northern cultures also placed trees in the midst of their customs and language. In all the Celtic languages, the word "trees" translates into English as "learning." Also, the Irish Druids of 1600 B.C. used an oral tree alphabet which formed a tree calendar. This alphabet, used for divination, consisted of five vowels and thirteen consonants.[2]

Trees in Mythology

Trees also are common symbols in mythology. In author James Frazer's "The Golden Bough," the opening story describes a sacred tree guarded by a priest of Diana at Aricaia in ancient Italy.

The ancient Greeks and Romans also held a belief that humans were the fruit of the ash tree. In Dodona, one of the oldest of the Greek sanctuaries, the god Zeus was worshipped as the form taken by a sacred oak, which was consulted as an oracle. Zeus' responses to

"What we see fit to save now will be all that is left of the work of the forces that some of us call God."

John Livingston

queries were interpreted from the rustling of the oak's leaves and murmur of the water that arose from a spring at the foot of this great giant.

The Tree as an Art Medium

Embracing the tree as an art medium presents the artist with a continually changing sculpture that transforms itself from season to season, year to year, from bare branch to full-leaf to flower and fruit. Each year brings added growth in the tree's diameter and height, which adds to the natural transformation of the creation.

The idea that trees could be shaped into works of art is not new. A friend of Julius Caesar's is credited with creating the first topiary through the careful shaping of shrubs. Later, the art of bonsai was embraced by the Japanese, who followed the Chinese practice of dwarfing trees.

Indeed, as people

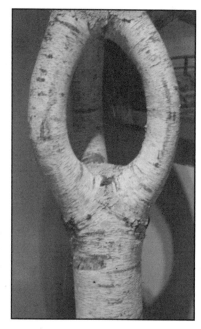

A preserved remnant of Axel Erlandson's Birch Loop tree is on permanent display in the Santa Cruz, Calif., museum.

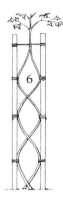

became interested in the aesthetics of trees, they consciously began to place structure upon their landscape.

Such man-designed structures were lavishly carried out on a grand scale throughout Europe and the growing communities of North America. Roads and pathways were straight, planting beds of rigid geometrical shape and limbs of tall trees gracefully swept against the backdrop of expansive sky. The gardens of Versailles best show these artful displays of uniform and symmetrical plantings as do the terraced gardens of the Italian Villa Lante at Bagnaia .

It is this desire to shape plant forms that has become the basis for a number of tree-shaping techniques developed and practiced by cultures around the world.

Topiary

Shaping through shearing is the best way to describe the art of topiary.

Whimsical garden sculpture creations - greenery swans seeming to swim across the waves of an undulating hedge. Teddy bears, dinosaurs, umbrellas - all are created through the careful clipping of evergreen shrubs.

> "The grandeur of life in our flowering world lies in its infinite possibilities."
>
> Rutherford Platt

First practiced during Roman times, topiary was introduced by Cnaius Matius, a friend of emperor Julius Caesar,

and soon the art flourished in the gardens of the well-to-do.

Following the fall of the Roman empire, topiary nearly vanished from common practice until eventually reappearing during the Italian Renaissance, where topiary techniques became more refined. Formal gardens sported neatly-trimmed geometrically-shaped shrubs and grassy avenues lined by close-cropped yew or boxwood hedges.[3]

Topiary shaping techniques are similar to those used to prune and shape a hedge to encourage dense growth. Once a shape is obtained, it is then trimmed at least twice a year to maintain its appearance.

Greenery sculptures also are created by training fast-growing plants such as ivy or a spreading rosemary over a moss-filled wire

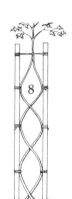

frame. The plants are then trimmed to closely follow the shape of the frame.

Bonsai

It is believed that more than 1,000 years ago, the Japanese were inspired by the Chinese practice of growing small trees to recreate the intricate beauty of naturally dwarfed trees. The art began with the collecting of small tree specimens with growth habits distorted by wind and poor growing conditions. As it developed, the art of bonsai, pronounced 'bones-sigh,' progressed to where young, nursery-grown trees are trained at the hands of a master pruner who artificially dwarfs trees and shrubs by clipping and contorting a plant's top growth while restraining roots to help control growth in the container which serves as the plant's home. Some of these traditional bonsai have lived for hundreds of years, with the individual plants passed on from generation to generation.

The art of bonsai begins with woody-stemmed plants with hardy, tapering trunks and small-leafed branches. The artist prunes and shapes the plant with the aim of creating a container plant that resembles a full-sized tree and landscape, thus bringing a bit of nature into the bonsai enthusiasts life. The number of trees and the placement within their container are important aesthetic decisions that are made by the bonsai master.

Today, bonsai not only is a way to create living art, it can be an affordable way to develop pruning techniques. A cast-off, root-bound juniper in the bone yard of a local nursery can be turned, with time and practice, into a classic bonsai for under $10, including the cost of potting soil and traditional bonsai container.

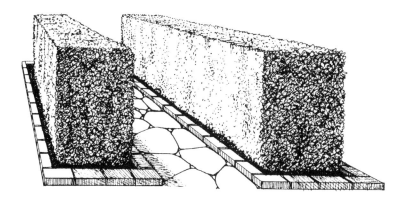

Hedges and Mazes

For some, a garden is not a garden without a hedge. Such lines of trees or clipped shrubs serve to divide the garden, neatly slicing up garden space into "rooms" for privacy or to create contrasting garden design.

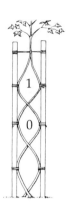

Hedges came into being as living fences to separate the garden from the pasture. As the landscape was formalized, the structure was neatly clipped to bring the unruly growth under control. Typical evergreen shrubs used for hedges include boxwood, privet and yew.

A hedge grown into a puzzle pattern is a maze. This living labyrinth is believed to have originated in 1600 B.C. with the maze created to enclose the Cretan Minotaur. Later, the maze came to symbolize the path of Christian pilgrims to Jerusalem. Mazes also became popular amusements during the Renaissance and later times and remain popular in European public gardens where visitors delight in traipsing through often confusing configurations of hedges.

Espalier

Small fruit trees are typically the prime candidates for the art of espalier, a shaping technique developed in the walled-cities of Europe as a way to raise crops in marginally warm regions.

"The real voyage of discovery consists not in seeking new landscapes, but in having new eyes."
                    Marcel Proust

Espalier is the training of the tree's branches to grow in a flat, vertical plane, typically against the south side of a building or wall where the trees receive protection as well as radiated warmth from the structure. Today, many orchardists seeking to increase production are espaliering their fruit trees along wire-supported rows as a way to obtain higher yields in a reduced amount of space.

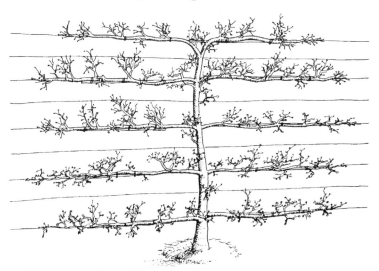

Over the years, espalier has expanded out of the fruit production world to include ornamental shrubs such as pyracantha and cotoneaster. Such ornamental plantings are well-suited to narrow areas, such as a planting bed between a

walkway and wall. The plants are then kept clipped flat against the wall to prevent the the plant from intruding upon those strolling by.

Pleaching

Similar to espalier is the technique of pleaching. Like espalier, pleaching trains rows

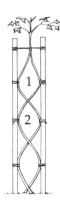

of trees to grow in a vertical, continuous plane. The difference is that pleached trees are free-standing away from the support of a wall or other structure. Also, the tree trunks are kept bare for a height of four to five feet with the branches gracefully woven into each other with extraneous growth clipped short to create a solid hedge that appears to be rising above the ground on stilts.

The technique, which also is referred to as plashing, began to appear in formal gardens in the 16th century as a way to create linked

avenues within the garden design.
Today, pleaching continues to be
found in formal gardens, often in
planting beds where the mature line of
interwoven and hedged trees is
underplanted with flowering bulbs
and annuals.

Trees with flexible growth and a
tolerance for shaping work best.Young
trees should be of uniform size and
shape and are planted eight to 12 feet apart. To
initiate the shaping, a wire framework is often
used, with a bottom wire placed at the intended
level for the lowest interwoven branches.
Additional wires are added above for the
training of the horizontal branches. Shoots
which cannot be trained into the horizontal

plane are trimmed
back to the trunk.
Later, when the shape
of the pleached hedge
is obtained, the
training wires can be
removed.

Grafting

It seems logical to
assume that the

**With two years of
growth following
grafting, these quaking
aspens are joined for
life.**

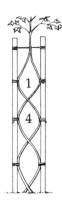

techniques of grafting - the joining of plant stems - came about from the observation of trees that naturally join in the course of their lives. Here, a branch may come in contact with that of a compatible neighbor and, over time, the two limbs will graft themselves into a single branch.

The particular technique called "approach grafting" is likely the first style of grafting practiced by early horticulturists. The first inhabitants of Mesopotamia grafted trees using this method, as did the Chinese before 2000 B.C.[4] More detailed information on grafting is provided in a later section on techniques.

Arborsculpture

Tree trunk topiary, botanical architecture, arbortopia - all of these terms have attempted to describe an early 1900s approach to tree shaping that goes beyond such traditional practices of topiary, bonsai and espalier.

Tree trunk topiary is unlike all other techniques. And so it needs a term like no other. I call it Arborsculpture.

While landscape topiary depends upon the shaping of foliage through careful pruning, the art of Arborsculpture uses the grafting of stems and limbs to create solid, ornamental and utilitarian structures. Imagine four vertical walls of grafted tree branches grown into a three dimensional house. Such a structure gives new meaning to the term "living room."

Unlike the other tree-manipulation methods, Arborsculpture utilizes a tree's inherent structure and growth pattern to create the finished form. The innovator of this new art was Axel Erlandson

In the 1920s, Erlandson, on his farm in Turlock, California, began shaping what to this day are considered the most outstanding

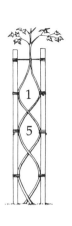

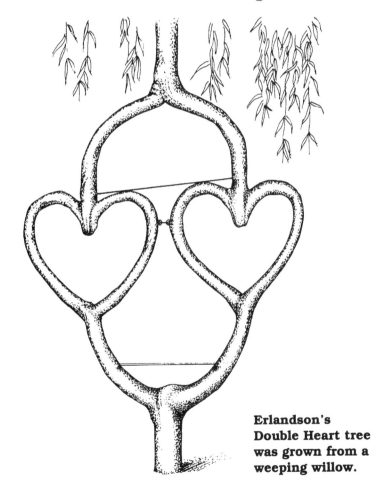

Erlandson's Double Heart tree was grown from a weeping willow.

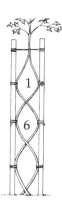

examples of tree trunk topiary in the world. Erlandson used techniques of multiple plantings, grafting, bending, and pruning to achieve his artistic and functional goals. It is his achievements that have inspired this book.

Axel Erlandson grew his Ladder Tree from two box elders. All nine rungs could be climbed

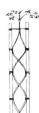
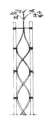

CHAPTER TWO

A xel Erlandson was an artist whose chosen medium was the live tree trunk. Over his lifetime, he created more than 70 mature Arborsculpture specimens that demonstrate his unique creativity.

Erlandson was born in 1884, the son of Swedish immigrants. He was just 18 years old when he and his family moved from their Minnesota home to the warmer climes of the West Coast where Erlandson lived much of his life on a modest farm surrounded by his family. There, he honed agricultural and other practical skills. For example, though he had a fourth-grade formal education, he taught himself the craft of surveying as a way to help solve drainage problems in his fields.

He also became a gifted grafter. While on his farm, he observed a natural graft between two sycamores that inspired him to create grafted trees of his own.

Erlandson's ambitions - and Arborsculptures - became larger over time. His creations, from spiral staircases, to a double heart weeping willow and a towering Cathedral window, exemplify the

> "All things move in music and write it. The mouse, lizard, grasshopper sing together on the Turlock sands, sing with the morning stars."
>
> John Muir

possibilities unleashed through imaginative shaping and grafting.

Nowhere on earth have trees been sculpted to such extent as those Erlandson grew for his park, The Tree Circus, which he opened to the public adjacent his Scotts Valley, California, home in 1947. Here, in his unusual roadside exhibit, Erlandson shared his Arborsculpture creations with the public.

This commercial enterprise, though, had its roots in Erlandson's agricultural upbringing. In the mid-1920s, Erlandson began shaping trees as a hobby away from the work at his Turlock bean farm, located in California's Central Valley, some 100 miles south of Sacramento.

Mark Primack, a Santa Cruz, Calif., architect and author of a manuscript on Erlandson's life, is perhaps the most knowledgeable authority on the Tree Circus, having documented Erlandson's trees in 1978, with grant funds from the California Arts Council. In 1994, Primack gave a public lecture on the Tree Circus to the Santa Cruz Historical Society before a standing-room-only crowd. Much of the information here was gathered from that talk.

Erlandson's first Arborsculpture experiment involved the planting of four sycamores in a six-foot square near the road by his Turlock farmhouse. Erlandson gradually pulled the limber tips of these young trees together, grafting them into a single "trunk" to form a pergola-like living structure that he later called the "Four Legged Giant."

Other creations soon followed. Erlandson would first draw his tree designs to scale on paper, plant the required number of trees, then create scaffolding structures to help train the young trees into shape. Some designs, such as the "Cathedral Window," took up to seven years to complete. The length of time to finish a design was often determined by the height Erlandson wanted his completed creation to be.

Most of Erlandson's sculptures were formed from the limber tree species of sycamore and box elder. He also utilized other species including willow, poplar, ash, birch, alder, loquat and apple.

Although bending and grafting were his basic techniques, Erlandson carefully guarded all that he learned about

The Needle and Thread Tree now resides in Gilroy, Calif.

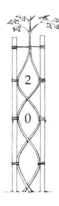

tree shaping. According to his daughter, Wilma, when a visitor asked how he shaped his trees, he would simply reply: "I talk to them." No records or notes were kept so speculation is the best we can offer.

Like a sleuth with a magnifying glass, I searched the old photos of Erlandson's trees, looking not at the photo's subject, but rather, the young framed trees that often appeared in the background. Later photos would often include these same trees. Thus, by comparing how these trees changed over time, I could get a real feel for how the tree grew and the trials that it endured.

For example, one photo sequence indicates a storm broke off the top of Erlandson's "Double Spectacle" tree. Erlandson apparently attempted to repair the damage, as indicated by later photos, but finally gave up the challenge. Photos taken even later appear to show that the loops on the Double Spectacle Tree died. Evidently, the tree's nutrients by-passed these loops in favor of a more direct nutrient route from root to crown.

Through deduction, it appears that this nutrient route was utilized only while the tree was young. Over time, as the tree's diameter increased, some sections of the design began to naturally graft, redirecting nutrient flow. This seems to illustrate the need for keeping an open-spaced design to ensure longevity of the Arborsculpture.

Inspection reveals that 3/8 inch metal bars were used to brace weak sections of this design. Still, the necessity of these braces is suspect. Erlandson only used the bars for three of the four loops. The loop that was not braced with a bar appears to have grown just as well as the braced sections.

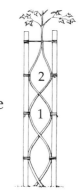

Erlandson, himself, seemed surprised at the success of his work. In a 1955 article in the Santa Cruz Sentinal, he was quoted as saying: "You would think that as the trees grow, the formation would change. But they don't. Branches will get larger in circumference, but the shape will remain about the same."

Another benefit of reviewing Erlandson's trees, comparing younger to older works over time, is that the oldest trees appear to have "swallowed" the evidence of previous grafts. By looking at early photos of these trees, it's possible to reconstruct the methods used to create the design.

Erlandson crafted an estimated 28 arboreal sculptures at his Turlock farm, including the impressive "Cathedral Window," formed from the careful grafting of 10 young trees, planted in a row, that eventually towered more than 20 feet

"... move along those shades. In gentleness of heart; with gentle hand Touch - for there is a spirit in the woods."

William Wordsworth

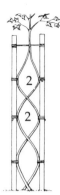 tall and included archway windows and a door. Still, as incredible as his creations were, few people except those in his local community who knew of his work, viewed his wonders.

But by the late-1940s, this would change. In 1945, Erlandson's wife Leona and then-teenaged daughter Wilma took a summer drive to the coastal town of Santa Cruz. There, they toured a popular roadside attraction called

Erlandson's Cathedral Window was planted in the 1920's at his Turlock, California, farm.

"The Mystery Spot." Leona and Wilma were impressed by the number of people willing to pay 25 cents each to see such oddities as tilted buildings and other optical illusions at The Mystery Spot. Upon returning home, they convinced Axel that his unique arboreal skills could be of even more interest to curious travelers.

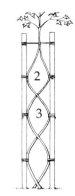

By then, at the age of 60, Erlandson was ready to leave farming behind and begin a new career. He quickly purchased a 3/4 acre parcel in Scotts Valley, six miles north of Santa Cruz, for a reported $1,050. Here, where the main road to the Pacific Coast crossed by his property, Erlandson set about the task of transplanting the hardiest of his Turlock trees to his new park land.

Erlandson carefully selected which of his Turlock trees - some of which were more than 20 years old - for transplant. Those chosen for the move were dug, bare-rooted, and then their foliage severely pruned to reduce transplant shock. Because the trees were so vulnerable to the weather at that time, they were kept wrapped in burlap for their truck trip over the coastal mountains to Scotts Valley.

Those trees which could not be successfully transplanted, Erlandson cut down and moved to Scotts Valley as well. These were propped up as "filler" trees at the park until Erlandson could replace them with live, similarly-sculpted trees.

In the spring of 1947, Erlandson open his

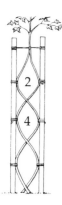

new park under the not-so humble banner proclaiming "See the World's Strangest Trees Here." It wasn't long, though, at daughter Wilma's suggestion, that the name was changed to "The Tree Circus."

Adjacent the attraction, Erlandson built a castle-shaped home for his family. Visitors could ring a bell to summon Erlandson from his work, and he'd then open the doors for his guests.

In the beginning, the Erlandsons were hardly overwhelmed with business. A "good" year would bring an average of four visitors a day to the Tree Circus. Publicity was needed to let the world know of Erlandson's creations.

To help advertise his Tree Circus, Erlandson began to distribute photographs of his creations. In a June 1947 letter to Robert Ripley, Erlandson noted that "Many people, including a couple nurserymen, have told me they have never seen trees like them anywhere else."

Ripley liked the photos enough that he published sketches of several of them in his famous "Believe It or Not!" newspaper column some 10 times from the late 1940s through the mid-1950s, and small publications began to take notice.

> "A great teacher never strives to explain her vision; she simply invites you to stand beside her and see for yourself."
> Rev. R. Inman

Erlandson's big break,

though, came when Life Magazine published an article in its Jan. 14, 1957 issue. The two page layout displayed photos of his trees, noting that "...they beat anything in the gardens of Versailles." Business quickly doubled.

With all the attention, Erlandson was approached by a wealthy European princess who asked to buy his trees and transplant them to her lavish estate. But Erlandson refused, noting that his customers would likely miss any removed trees.

Still, Erlandson was growing older and realized that the work of his "Tree Circus" was growing more difficult. In the early 1960s, he contacted the California State Parks Department, inquiring whether it would be interested in taking over his enterprise. The response, though, was a friendly "no thank you."

In 1963, Erlandson sold the property and his trees to a retired real estate agent from the San Francisco Bay area, who purchased the business for his son to operate. Erlandson died a year later.

By the early 1960s, tourism traffic was being routed off of Scotts Valley Drive to the new, nearby Highway 17, leaving Scotts Valley Drive as a frontage highway with greatly reduced traffic. The new Tree Circus owner, reasoning he could perhaps attract more visitors by expanding the attraction, erected large plastic dinosaurs that could be seen from the new

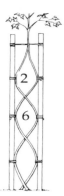

highway. He also renamed the roadside attraction "The Lost World." But "The Lost World" would only last some 14 years, eventually closing its doors in 1977. By now, the precious trees began to be neglected.

Again, the property changed hands, this time being sold to a landscaper who intended to move the unusual trees to Southern California where they could be sold. Though the new owner had already begun the two-year process of preparing the trees for another transplant, Primack and others were able to convince him that the trees, and the attraction, were worth saving.

It was now the early 1980s and the trees were suffering from neglect. Drought also was beginning to take its toll and a developer had other uses for the property in mind. It

Myray Many Moons Reames stands inside the Telephone Booth. The tree, which was cut in May 1995, has been stripped of bark to prevent further decay of its wood.

was then that Michael Bonfante, owner of Nob Hill Foods and a local nursery in Gilroy, Calif., purchased the remaining trees.

In 1985, Bonfante's crews boxed and moved the survivors some 50 miles south to be part of Bonfante's planned 75-acre amusement park. In all, 28 of Erlandson's masterpieces were successfully transplanted under Bonfante's care. Additionally, portions of specimens that had died are preserved by a Santa Cruz, Calif., museum. Six remain at the original Scotts Valley Tree Circus site while one creation, called "The Telephone Booth" by Erlandson, was cut in the spring of 1995 by Mark Primack and prepared for its new home at the American Visionary Art Museum in Baltimore, Md..

When Axel Erlandson died in 1964 at the age of 79, there were an estimated 75 living sculptures still gracing the grounds of the Tree Circus. These included a spiral staircase, a ladder, an intricate honeycomb-shaped structure and several towers.

Erlandson's life's work has now been scattered to new homes for appreciation by a wider public. As a result, new interest is being cultivated today to carry on the art of Arborsculpture as pioneered by Axel Erlandson.

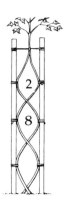

2
8

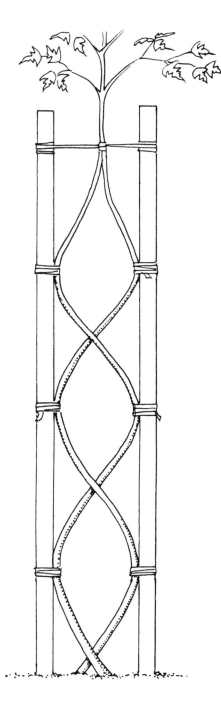

This is one way the
Oliver Twist tree
may have been
shaped .

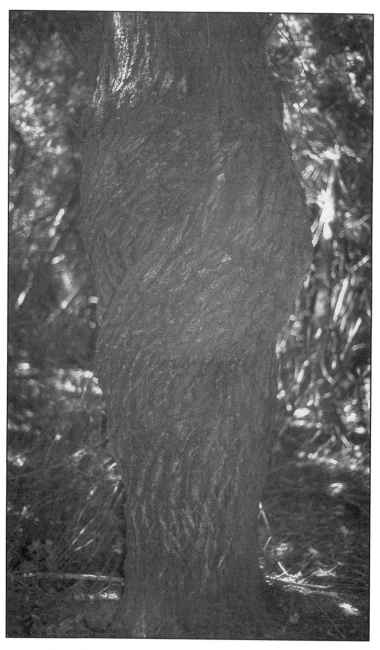

The Oliver Twist Tree photographed in 1995 at
the former site of The Tree Circus in Scotts Valley.

Erlandson in his home-grown chair in December, 1954. Erlandson had his own techniques for growing chairs. This particular one was created from four trees.

In 1947, The Tree Circus opens with newly transplanted trees along with some filler trees that have been cut and moved from Erlandson's Turlock farm. These filler trees are propped up beside the newly-transplanted specimens. Admission to The Tree Circus was 25 cents.

Erlandson with his Totem Tree, 1954.

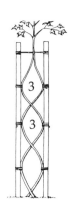

This photograph of the Tepee Tree was taken in 1954. Today, it is part of the Hecker Pass Family Park.

The Sycamore Tower was featured in a January 14, 1957 article in Life Magazine. This photo was taken in 1967

Standing underneath the Nine-toed Giant is
Billy Queally in this 1995 photo at the former
Tree Circus.

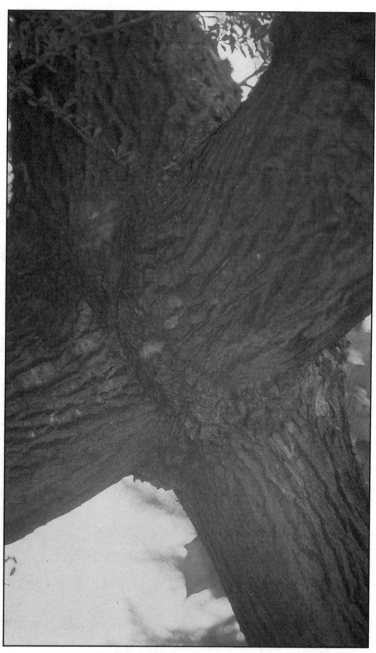

The underview of the Nine-toed Giant shows
where the three trunks have been grafted together.

A curlicued branch was created by Erlandson on
this specimen that now is part of the
Hecker Pass Family Park.

This Erlandson tree resembles the letter H.

A spiral staircase was created from two trees.

Branches shaped to form right angles help give
this tree its name: The Revolving Door Tree.

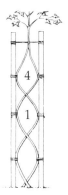

A Double Corkscrew is formed from a box elder.

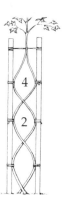

The Four-Legged Giant is shaped from four trees.

The Archway Tree is created from two
grafted sycamores.

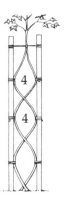

A single tree is designed through intricate grafting to create six diamonds.

The Four-Ringed Tree has retained healthy loops
over several decades of growth.

The Figure Eight Tree is formed from two trees.

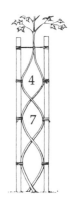

A Zig-Zag Tree is created from a single poplar.

**One tree becomes four trunks then returns to a
single trunk in this specimen.**

The sycamore 'Double Spectacle' Tree in 1995.
This tree also can be seen in the Tree Circus'
Opening Day photo on page 31.

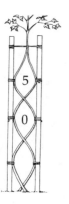

5

0

Two hearts mirror each other in this vertical version of Erlandson's Double Heart tree.

The Loop-de-loop Tree.

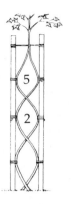

Joy Boy Magic Maker stands inside Erlandson's Sycamore Tower tree, which is now located at the Hecker Pass Family Park.

CHAPTER THREE

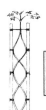 

Arborsmith Studios is a tree nursery specializing in Tree Trunk Topiary - the creative shaping of tree trunks. Simply put, this shaping is called Arborsculpture.

In 1990, as I found myself facing fatherhood, I sincerely prayed for a career that would support my new family, benefit the earth and satisfy my creative urges. Images of Erlandson's trees entered my mind and Arborsmith Studios was born.

For years, I have been intrigued by the trees of Axel Erlandson. As a boy, I visited his Scotts Valley Tree Circus with my family. And because I was just a youngster, I didn't appreciate the work as much then as I do now. Still, the sight of Axel's oddly-shaped trees stuck with me.

My calling was clear: While I was in college, I focused on horticulture and botany. The prospects of grafting piqued my interest and I realized I could make a contribution to this art form. I am writing this book to encourage more experiments into this art medium because so little is really known about this expansive subject. My aim is to inspire and instruct artists and gardeners in the use of Erlandson's medium to enhance their landscapes

"In the woods we return to reason and faith."

Ralph Waldo Emerson

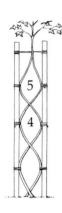

and gardens.

Beginning my research, I went to the site of the former Tree Circus and found seven of Axel's trees still remaining. I also contacted Erlandson's daughter Wilma who graciously shared photos and insights into her life at The Tree Circus.

I also began to do some experimenting on my own. During my first experiments in 1987, I attempted to create my own Arborsculptures using approach grafts on manzanita limbs. Also, I planted seven fruit trees together in a tight circle to prepare for approach grafts that, according to my plan, would

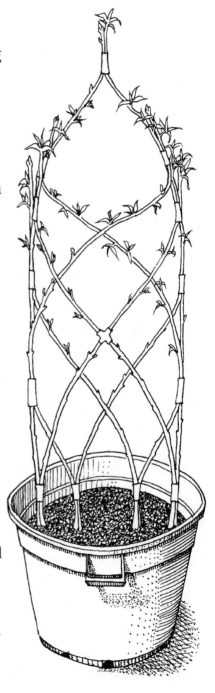

eventually create a garden gazebo. Later, in 1991, I attempted grafting projects with a number of trees growing in the wild.

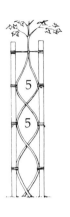

Like Erlandson, I took notice of nature. Naturally-grafted madrone trees on my forested property provided constant inspiration. Without any human help, nature can produce some amazing sculptures.

In the spring of 1992, I purchased a number of trees from a local nursery and began the shaping process. An early in-ground project began with six hybrid poplar trees, planted in two rows, three feet apart. The idea was to create a living archway.

Living in a rural area poses many challenges, with the presence of deer being one of the most vexing. It wasn't long before my poplars were badly damaged by deer. It appears they like to chew the tree bark to get at the soft cambium tissues. Four of the young trees were ruined so I removed them and caged the remaining two poplars with wire mesh to ward off further attack.

Next, I took the two survivors and began to bend and graft their stems in an unusual way. To create an arch, I grafted their stems together with their vascular systems going in opposite directions. Through this experiment I aimed to gain an understanding of the limits of grafting. Because

> "As the twig is bent, the mulberry grows."
> Ancient Chinese proverb

A Peace Sign crafted from a cherry tree in 1993.

the vascular systems are in opposition, theory has it that a graft would not be successful. Yet, as of this writing, the trees are healthy and a small ridge of tissue has grown, indicating that the two stems have successfully grafted. I suspect, though, that despite the successful graft, the vascular systems will remain at least in part separate.

Another project began with a cherry seedling purchased at a Mother's Day plant sale. The seedling had been topped at a height of five feet and here, six branches shot out in all directions. These I bent and grafted into a living Peace Sign, shown in the photo on the previous page.

From studying Erlandson's work and through my experimentation, I've developed some theories as to why particular Arborsculpture techniques are more successful than others. To summarize:

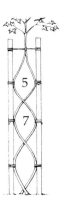

1 - Trees may be planted as close together as needed. When they are joined through grafting, they essentially become a single tree with an extended root system.

2 - Symmetrical designs that provide the tree with equally distant pathways from root to crown are most likely to remain symmetrical in design as the trees continue to grow. Should a portion of the design outgrow another portion, the fast-growing section can be slowed through the Arborsculpture techniques of ring barking and scoring, more completely described in Chapter 4.

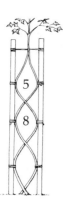

3 - The shape of a tree's trunk is created by firmly securing it into the desired position long enough to "cast" this position into permanent form.

Through my experiments, I've become more confident designing tree trunk topiary. So in the spring of 1993, with the image of Erlandson sitting in his unique Arborsculpted chair, I began to sculpt a set of living chairs, complete with woven seats. Formed from a number of species, including apple and alder, these chairs now vary from doll-size to specimens large enough to seat an adult.

Other experiments that are ongoing at Arborsmith Studios incorporate the technique of inclusion. This is where an object such as a crystal, or even a mailbox or bird cage, is 'included' in the tree sculpture in such a way that the tree, through its growth, slowly swallows the object and incorporates it into its structure.

A twist on this idea is to create naturally-formed tool handles with the help of the tree. For example, an old tool head can be slipped over a branch, and with enough growth, the branch will eventually fill the handle opening in the tool head. Then, the branch can be removed and the branch becomes the new handle for your tool.

Obviously, creating

> "If it can live, then let it live."
>
> Ken Carey, referring to business practices of the future

such a tool takes a bit of time. And the
question I'm most often asked is: "Does
tree sculpturing take a lot of patience?
In response, I like to tell people that
"you only need patience if you live in
the future. The key is to live in the
now."

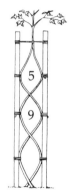

Depending upon your design, an
Arborsculpture can take from two
months to 10 years or more to
complete. Tall, complicated designs using slow-
growing trees will take many years to mature.
Successful grafts can heal in as short a time as
two months during rapid spring growth, but
will take longer during slower growth periods in
the fall and winter. And intricate projects such
as living chairs may take two to three years to
develop sufficient strength to support the
weight of an adult.

Arborsculpture also can be performed on a
miniature level by incorporating the basic
techniques of bonsai with grafting. Intriguing,
small sculptures, perfect for tabletop display,
are the result.

The initial design and grafting work on a
small project can take just one afternoon to
complete. This is as close as one can get to
"instant graftification."

I believe that the art of Arborsculpture will
change the rules and tools of the landscape as
we begin to create such outdoor enhancements
as fencing from live trees, living outdoor
furniture and even, enchanting children's
playhouses created from living trees.

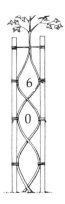

My dream project is to have a round acre of flat ground on which to design and grow a very special park.

This park would be encircled with a dense hedge and at the entrance, located in the East, I'd create a maze of flowering trees. Once inside, visitors will find a sculptural arboretum and a path circling to the South. Along the pathway at the west side of the garden will be a house created from living trees and furnished with living furniture. Behind the house, an orchard would be planted with a variety of fruit trees whose trunks are shaped into ladders, making for easy fruit picking.

There also would be a children's play area, including a jungle gym crafted from trees. In the middle of the park will stand a peaceful pool of water. There, a graceful waterfall would spill from a

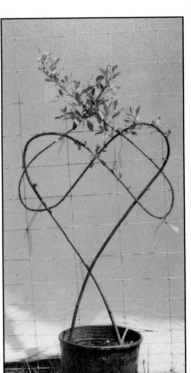

At Arborsmith Studios, two willows are woven into a Celtic knot.

weeping willow into the pond.

People interacting with their landscape - this is the most inspiring aspect of Arborsculpture.

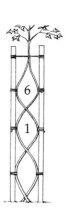

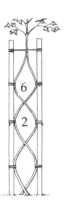

A Walk-Through Tree, at right, is the result of an experiment to graft opposing vascular systems with hybrid poplar. Below, a table and two chairs are examples of living lawn furniture.

The back of a cherry chair shows off the intricate designs that can be achieved.

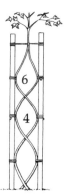

A Wall of Diamonds, at right, is created from eight poplars planted in a container. Below, a spiral table is shaped from red alder.

Myray Many Moons Reames with her own
poplar chair.

Richard Reames brings together the top
section to form the back of a red alder chair
while the trees are still dormant.

M ost tree growth originates from the stem tips in an area called the apical bud, as shown in the illustration. Many trees exhibit a phenomenon called "apical dominance," where the shoot tip grows and produces a hormone that inhibits the growth of the lower buds. Some trees have weak apical dominance, which allows shoots to grow from each leaf axil soon after they are formed.

Apical bud

To understand how a tree grows, you have to take a look inside. In the cross section of a tree trunk shown in the illustration on the next page, these parts of the tree can be clearly seen as rings of tissue.

On the exterior of the tree is the bark, which helps protect the tree's interior from weather and attack from insects and animals.

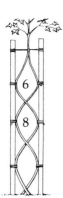

Next is the phloem, which is part of the tree's vascular system, carrying sugars - the tree's food - in a downward direction. As the tree grows, the thin cell walls of phloem become crushed, and eventually become part of the tree's bark.

The cambium is the next layer, and this is where the tree produces its new cells. This layer is just a few cells in width and can make a new layer of phloem and

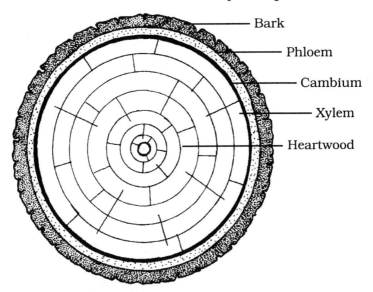

- Bark
- Phloem
- Cambium
- Xylem
- Heartwood

xylem each year. This cell development is what causes rings to form in a tree, which if counted, can help determine the tree's age.

The next layer of tissue is the xylem, which transport nutrients, water and the growth hormones called cytokinins upward in the tree from the roots to the leaves. At the center is the heartwood. These were once living cells, but now have become the structural support for the tree.

It's important to understand the fluid dynamics of a tree to understand how to successfully create Arborsculpture designs through grafting, pruning and ring barking.

For example, when there is more than one route for the flow of a tree's fluids, some tree species send fluids through the route that is most direct from its roots to leaf canopy and from leaf canopy to roots. Those routes which are less direct will receive less, or more radically, no nutrient-filled fluids. Eventually, these routes will grow slowly or even die.

But this effect differs from tree species to species. Some trees will try to keep alive all viable fluid routes while others will give up these routes readily.

To use the tree's fluid dynamics to help shape your Arborsculpture, you can remove strips of bark from selected limbs. For example, to prevent a branch from becoming more dominant than the others, remove a small strip of bark to equalize the flow of nutrients to all the branches. Four methods of altering growth through bark removal are shown in the following illustration.

"I believe the right question to ask, respecting all ornament, is simply this: Was it done with enjoyment - was the carver happy while he was about it?"

John Ruskin

Ring Barking

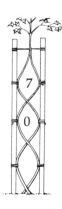

This illustration shows the five methods for impeding the movement of nutrients in the phloem. The normal time to perform these techniques is in the early summer. By manipulating the bark, you promote flower buds, slow vegetative growth and reduce root activity the following year

1 - Removal of an incomplete bark ring, 2 cm or 3/4 of an inch wide, leaving a bridge of bark.

2 - Removal of a sprial strip of bark forces some lateral movement of phloem.

3 - The phloem is just below the bark and can be scored with a knife.

4 - Ring inversion. A strip of bark 2 cm or 3/4 of an inch wide is removed then immediately replaced, upside down. A plastic stretch tiesecures the bark in place. The technique forces the phloem to produce new cells in the correct orientation.

5 - Removal of a complete ring of bark, 1 cm or 3/8 inch wide.

NOTE: Use only one technique on a branch at a time. Scoring is easiest for the beginner

1

2

3

4

5

Selecting trees for Arborsculpture

Trees add more than shade to a landscape. They provide shelter from wind, noise and curious neighbors. They're a source of food and flowers, attracting birds and butterflies to the garden. And interesting bark and growth habits provide variation and diversity in the garden scheme.

Almost any tree can be used for tree-trunk topiary, although some species are less suitable than others. For example, sumac is a poor choice because its stems are rather short-lived. Some conifers have compact growth and stiff stems that make them more difficult to shape.

It is wise to study the particular growing culture and habits of the trees you work with. For example, coastal redwoods tend to naturally shed their lower branches as they mature. Therefore, Arborsculpture designs utilizing lower branches on a redwood are doomed to failure from the start.

Perhaps most importantly, because of the time you'll invest in your project, it's best to choose tree species that will grow well in your climate and fit the location you choose. Avoid planting tall-growing trees under utility lines and take care you don't plant your sculptures where they may block your favorite views.

Species that may work for you include:

Willow (Salix spp.)
Alder (Alnus)
Poplar (Populus)
Maple (Acer)
Apple (Malus)
Birch (Betula)
Ash (Fraxinus)
Eucalyptus
Plum (Prunus)
Cherry (Prunus)
Sycamore (Platanus)
Box elder (Acer)

Plant material for your project doesn't have to be expensive. If purchasing trees, especially in large quantity, bare root trees are the most inexpensive. These should be planted from fall through early spring and kept well watered during their first summer season.

Bareroot trees also can be planted into containers where they can develop a larger root system before they are planted in their permanent location during the fall and winter.

Also, there are some free sources for trees. When I first began to experiment with tree shaping, I went to the nearby forests to find trees on which to experiment with shaping techniques. There, I worked with the oaks, madrones, fir and pine.

Rules regarding use of public forests vary, so it's best to check with your local officials to avoid the embarrassment of being confronted by them while you're in the act of some odd tree contortions.

Still better, you can create your own trees by propagating and growing your own. Willows and poplars root readily and cuttings often can be obtained from friends or neighbors just for the asking.

The trick is to find suitable cuttings with the proper stem size, from about 1/4 inch to 1/2 inch in diameter, that will easily bend. The cuttings of these species can easily be rooted in water, although I've found that hybrid poplar cuttings will root readily when stuck directly into moist soil. The length of the cutting also has little effect on its ability to root, with whips up to eight feet long rooting satisfactorily.

If you have a source of young seedlings, transplanting these into containers will offer inexpensive trees for shaping. I've successfully transplanted young maples into containers by digging them from a nearby forest in mid-winter. Broken roots should be carefully trimmed away and the tops of the young trees pruned to keep a balance between the root ball and the top of the plant it will support.

Planting Your Trees

Some people like to use the phases of the moon as a planting guide. For moon watchers, the best time to plant trees is in the third quarter of the moon's cycle as the moon is waning. The best moon signs of the Zodiac for

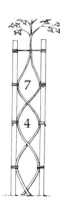

planting trees are considered to be Taurus, Cancer, Scorpio, Pisces, Capricorn and Leo.[1]

As previously mentioned, bare root trees should be planted when they are dormant, from December through March. Planting containerized or balled and burlapped trees can be done at any time, but care should be taken prevent roots from drying out during the planting process.

The prime season to plant, though, is early winter. This gives the tree a chance to grow a healthy root system before the dry, summer season hits and places your sculpted tree under additional stress. Also, the hole you dig should be three to five times the width of the root ball and add some good compost to the hole before placing your tree. When backfilling the hole, make sure the tree stands at the same soil level as it did in the container, to avoid burying the plant too deeply, which can cause stem rot.

Framing

As you design your Arborsculpture, you also will design the frame that will train the sculpture to its final shape. The frame's purpose is to temporarily hold the form until the tree grows sufficiently to support the shape by itself.

Simple frames would include, for example, a fence, which could be used to train a two-dimensional design. The tree is bent and tied to the frame in the desired shape.

When framing a tree's shape, plastic stretch

Axel Erlandson built an elaborate frame to guide this tree's growth.

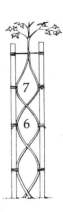

ties, which are available at most garden centers, can be used to pull a branch into place. Sometimes it is easier to push two branches apart. A notched block of wood can be squeezed between the branches, then positioned so that the notch holds the branch securely in place.

For framing material, a good scrap wood pile is the first place to search. Temporary frames can be made out of anything as long as the material serves the purpose of holding the tree into the desired shape. Even bamboo plant stakes, available at most hardware stores, are strong enough to support Arborsculpture designs.

Frame sections can be secured by many methods, including tying sections together with wire or securing them with wood screws. Avoid hammering nails into the frames as you may damage your tree as you later try to pry apart the nailed sections.

Pruning

Pruning can be an enjoyable task because it brings you into close, physical touch with your trees.

Pruning to stimulate a tree's growth is done during the winter months, while pruning to limit growth is done during summer months. Some species such as maple and birch, though, are best pruned during summer or in mid-winter because these species, when pruned during the spring, tend to bleed sap profusely.

When a large limb must be removed, use a sharp saw to prevent leaving jagged edges on your limb. A jagged cut will take longer to heal than a smooth cut.

To avoid tearing the bark on the underside of the limb, make a partial cut underneath the branch and close to the trunk. Then, make a second cut from the top of the branch to meet your first cut. Leave as short a stub as possible to encourage the wound to heal quickly. Pruning the branch with a sloping cut also helps rain water run off the surface, preventing rot from entering the cut's surface.

Smaller branches can be removed with pruning loppers or hand shears. Again, cuts should be made close to the main stem to encourage rapid healing.

During the spring and summer months, growth of side shoots can be checked by pinching them back with thumb and forefinger. When the tree is young, though, avoid removing too many lower branches. These will shade and protect the trunk and stems from sunburn.

A radical pruning technique is called pollarding. Though many arborists decry pollarding because of its stubby look, the technique allows an Arborsculpturist to

> "New opinions are always suspected and usually opposed, without any other reason but because they are not already common."
>
> John Locke

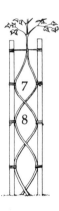

create grand designs in just a season or two.

Pollarding is accomplished during the winter months on mature trees. Main branches are pruned to the main trunk, leaving the tree looking much like a botanical "Venus de Milo."

What happens, though, is that during the following spring, the tree responds to the pruning by growing epicormic shoots, commonly called "water sprouts." These are long, flexible shoots which are easy to graft into shape. Additionally, the growth rate of the selected water sprouts can be promoted by pruning away the excess shoots not needed for your design.

Note that pollarding is an advanced technique that should be cautiously used only by experienced arborists to avoid permanent damage to the tree that could cause its demise.

As an aside, don't leave your pruning debris laying on the ground. This material may become a host for diseases and pests. It's best to gather your debris, chip and compost it to allow the heat of the composting process to destroy lingering pests.

Nicking and Notching

Nicking and notching are techniques used to eliminate unwanted buds or to encourage buds to sprout from the main stems of a plant. In both techniques, a small wedge of bark is removed from the stem. How the wedge is cut determines whether you are nicking or notching.

For example, nicking just below a bud will interrupt the flow of nutrients to the bud, preventing it from sprouting. Also, another quick way to prevent a bud from sprouting is to remove it completely by pinching it off before it can develop.

By contrast, notching above the bud will cause the nutrients to build up in the bud, forcing it to sprout. So if your sculpture needs a branch in a particular area, notching can stimulate a bud to grow, providing you with the needed branch.

Bending

The diameter of a limb and the species of tree will determine how far a branch or leader may be bent before it will break. With a little practice, you can get a feel for how radically you can bend a branch without damaging the tree. Don't be shy: You'll likely break a few branches in the learning process.

However, a broken branch often can be repaired. Place the branch back into its original position and bind the broken sections together

"In any weather, at any houre of the day, or night, I have been anxious to improve the nick of time, and notch it on my stick too; stand on the meeting of two eternities, the past and the future, which is precisely the present moment; to toe that line."

H. D. Thoreau

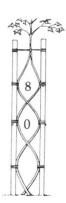

with the aid of a splint. The limb will eventually heal, although it will take a year or two of growth before the arboreal operation can be called a success.

More radical than bending is a technique called "creasing." The branches of some especially limber species, such as willow or poplar, can be folded over upon themselves without breaking.

Though you can bend and crease limbs with ease, it's not without resistance from the tree. When an upright branch is bent, the tree will attempt to counter-act the pressure by growing new xylem cells on the inside portion of the bend to force the branch back into its upright position. To overcome this natural "unbending" by the tree, the branch must be held in place for two or more years until enough new growth is formed to cast the shape permanently. Only then can you release the tree from its constraints.

In most cases the bud of a tree that is highest will grow the fastest. When a branch is bent down, changing the position of the leader bud, the tree may send out a new leader bud to domonate the flow of nutrients. These new leaders should be pruned back or tied down to channel the growth where you want it.

Some trees respond by self-pruning when a leader is bent downward. That is, the branch or its tip dies. To avoid this problem, always make sure the apical bud of the branch is upright. So, wait until the branch is long enough to be able to bend it horizontally, and also, be able to bend the apical bud back into a vertical position.

Grafting

Natural unions of tree parts are not uncommon in the world of horticulture. The most common place where a tree will create a natural graft is in its roots. It's been shown that neighboring trees of the same species will self-graft root tissue, creating an almost symbiotic relationship between the two trees. It's been observed that a tree stump will continue to grow with the aid of a neighboring tree, which has grafted its roots to those of the stump. The stump is, in effect, supported by the nutrients provided by its neighbor.

Other common natural grafts occur typically when a branch of one tree will lodge in the fork of limbs on a neighboring tree. Over time, the wind will push and pull the trees, rubbing raw the point where the tree branch hits the fork. As the trees naturally begin to heal their wounds, they will eventually graft themselves together with their newly formed tissue.

In the commercial fruit

"The mystery of esthetic like that of material creation is accomplished. The artist, like the god of the creation, remains within or behind or beyond or above his handiwork, invisible, refined out of existence, indifferent, paring his fingernails."
James Joyce

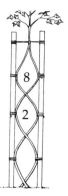

industry, grafting is commonly used to force a twig of one variety, called a scion, to grow on the root stock of another variety. The technique offers growers several advantages. For example, by using root stock from dwarf varieties, growers control the height of their fruit tree orchard, making for easier harvest. Fruit size, however, will be unaffected because the grower grafted a scion of a standard-sized fruit.

The more closely related the tree species, the more successful the grafts. Grafting within a species, such as one apple variety to another, is almost always successful. Grafts outside a species are possible, but frequently unsuccessful.

Grafting allows the tree sculptor to add branches at will. Grafting also allows the artist to change bark textures and colors within the sculpture. As example, birches are available in varieties with bark colors ranging from mahogany to white. By grafting different varieties together, bark colors can be intermingled to achieve truly unique Arborsculpture specimens.

Almost any manipulation that achieves cambial contact between the joined stems may produce a successful graft. And the possibilities are nearly endless. In his book, "The Grafters Handbook," R.J. Garner describes more than 50 grafting methods, each for a distinct application.

For Arborsculpture, though, the most useful

graft is one called an "approach graft." It is easy to learn and has a very high success rate. Its most distinguishing feature is that two self-sustaining trees, or portions of a tree, are wounded and secured together, allowing the graft to form as the wounds heal.

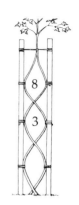

Here's a quick description and illustration of three approach graft methods.

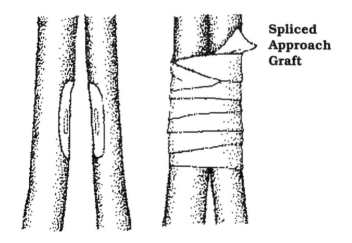

Spliced Approach Graft

Spliced Approach Graft

Two stems of approximately the same diameter are used in this method. At the point where the two stems will be joined, remove a slice of bark and wood from each stem. The cuts should be the same size so that the cambium patterns, when joined, will match. Also, the cuts should be smooth and flat, enabling close contact between the cambium layers. The cut surfaces of the stems are

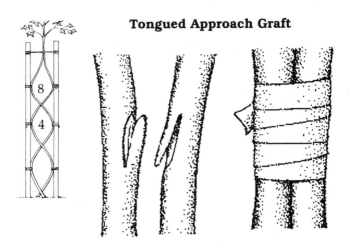

brought together and the two stems are bound tightly together with stretch ties.

Tongued Approach Graft.

   Though similar to the spliced approach graft, the tongued graft involves making a slanting cut into both pieces of stem. The cut on one stem is made in an upwards fashion while the cut on its graft-mate is in a downward fashion. The two pieces are slipped together to interlock tightly. The grafted section is then bound.

   (For what it's worth, this technique was demonstrated to me by Axel Erlandson in a dream!)

Inlay Approach Graft.

   This technique is used when one branch is large while the other is small. The idea is to "inlay" the smaller section into the larger to create the graft.

   The smaller branch is sliced smooth on one

Inlay Approach Graft

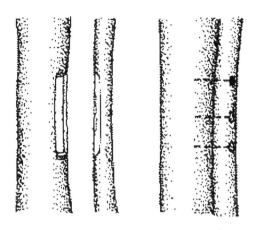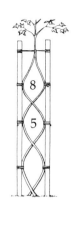

side. On both sides of this slice, a small cut is made, leaving a ridge between the main slice and the smaller cuts.

On the larger stem, two parallel cuts, the same length as those on the smaller stem, are made. The bark between these parallel cuts is then removed, leaving a slot about as wide as the cut you've made on the smaller stem. The wounded side of the small stem is then inserted into the cut on the larger branch. The graft section is then bound with stretch ties.

In some cases, a small nail can be used to help hold the large and small stems together. Drill a small hole for the nail, push it into place and cut off any portion of nail above the bark's surface. The drill hole should be slightly smaller than the size of the nail.

Approach grafting can be done at any time of the year, but the best results are obtained in early spring. For those following the lunar cycles, grafting is best done during a waxing moon.

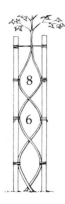

Other grafts

The bridge graft is another type of graft that may be useful for the Arborsculpturist. Normally, this technique is used to help save a tree that has been severely wounded, for example, one that has been girdled by animals or insects. Healthy shoots from the tree are cut and stored while the tree remains dormant. Then in early spring, the bottom portions of these scions are grafted to the tree below the wound. The scion tips are then bent over the wound and grafted into the healthy tissue above, effectively "bridging" the wounded area.The Arborsculpturist can then use these bridge grafts to create new limbs on the tree, bending and grafting both ends of the scion wood into the position and shape required for the sculpture.

Budding is another type of graft which can be used to add a branch where none previously existed. Budding, in which a single bud is inserted into the bark of the host tree, can also be used to change bark color or texture by inserting compatible yet contrasting scion wood into the sculpture.

Grafting is an art in itself, as noted by Oxford horticulturist Francis Drope. In 1672, Drope wrote:

"These are the chief ways of grafting, some whereof are necessary for a complete grafter to know, other some mere curiosities; but there are other variations which I purposely omit; supposing that from these, as from the chief heads, an ingenious lover of this art, will of his own industry, discover and improve them, to his greater pleasure and content."[3]

Tools and Wraps

The essential tool for grafting is a good quality grafting knife with a straight-edged blade that is strongly set in its

handle. If you prefer to use a folding knife, be sure it has a lock to keep it from closing on your hand.

Knives should be kept sharp to create clean cuts. And because they're sharp, use caution to prevent accidently cutting yourself.

A more versatile knife for Arborscultping, though, is one that comes with a handle and interchangeable blades. The blades are available in straight, rounded or pointed versions and can be inexpensively replaced when they become dull.

Pruning shears also are necessary to quickly

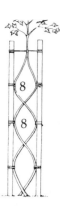

prune away unneeded stems and branches. Bypass shears work best because anvil types of shears tend to crush the plant's stem as they cut.

For detail pruning, bonsai scissors, which are used to prune miniature trees, may be helpful.

To prevent the spread of infection and disease, all knives and shears should be disinfected in a diluted bleach dip. Tools are then rinsed in clean water.

Other materials you'll need include wraps and white glue. These are used to limit the passage of air and water to wounds. Loosely wrapped white cloth bandages also can prevent sun scald on sensitive areas of the tree trunk.

Commercial black tree sealants aren't a good choice for a wrap because the tree is forced to grow around and swallow the sticky stuff as the wounds try to heal. Instead, I've used plastic tie strips as a wrap and then sealed the wrap with white glue. The glue peels off when the plastic tie strips are removed after the graft has healed.

Wraps should be made of stretchable materials such as fabric or plastic binding tape. These will stretch as the tree grows, preventing the tape from cutting into the tree. The wraps also should be of a light color so that they will reflect solar heat.

Periodically all stretch ties should be inspected,

> "I think that I shall never see, a poem as lovely as a tree. Poems are made by fools like me, but only god can make a tree."
>
> Joyce Kilmer

loosened and retied if necessary to avoid constriction.

When using plastic stretch ties, be careful to overlap the tape no more than half its width to avoid constricting the limb's growth. I use a sturdy stretch ribbon for tying branches into place and a lighter version for securing grafts.

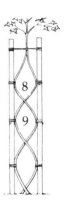

**Maya Many Moons Reames sees through
Erlandson's Arborsculpted acacia tree in this
1995 photo at the former Tree Circus.**

CHAPTER FIVE

Projects

The Fence

This is one of the easiest, as well as most practical, projects for the beginning grafter. Materials needed:

■ Pliable trees.
■ Plastic stretch ties.

1 - Determine the number of trees you'll need by the length of your desired fence. Each tree should be planted from six inches to two feet apart in a line.

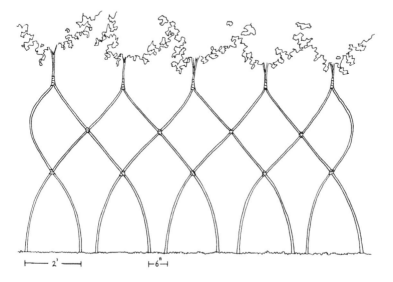

⊢— 2' —⊣   ⊢6"⊣

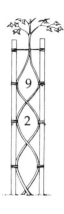

2 - Bend and cross the tree whips into the desired pattern. Where the tree limbs cross, create an approach graft, binding tightly with the plastic tape.

NOTE: By using a tight design and trees spaced no more than three feet apart, an almost solid wall can be grown in just a few years.

The Clockwise Twist

Materials needed:

■ Three or more trees, 5 foot tall whips of any tree species. Whips should be free of side branching.

■ Tree stakes, one for each tree planted. Stakes should be about 5 feet long.

■ Plastic stretch ties.

1 - Mark each stake at vertical intervals of one foot.

2 - Plant the young whips in a circle

3 - To the

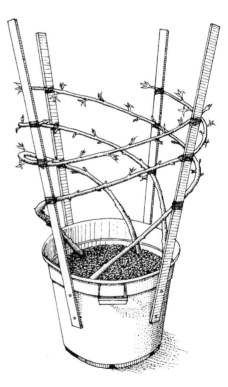

outside of the circle, install a stake behind each whip making sure the markings are all at the same height from the ground.

4 - Select a whip and gently bend it clockwise toward the next stake in the circle. Firmly tie the whip to this stake at the lowest marking point on the stake.

5 - Take the top of the same whip and again bend it clockwise to the next stake in the circle. Tie the whip firmly to this stake at the second lowest marking point.

6 - Continue bending and tying the whips in the same fashion until you run out of whips.

— Repeat steps 4,5 and 6 with the remaining whips.

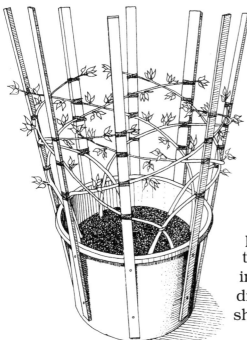

Want to create a counter-clockwise twist? Just train the trees in the opposite direction. Or, create a diamond pattern by training whips in opposite directions, as shown at left.

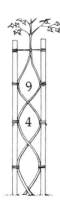

The Peace Sign

Materials needed:
■ One single-trunked tree with at least five pliable branches originating from about the same section of stem.
■ Plastic stretch ties.

1- Select the most vertical branch to create the center piece of the Peace Sign.
2 - Select the two branches closest to this center vertical branch for the two diagonal legs. Bend each to the center branch, grafting them to the center branch and bind the graft with the tape.
2 - The last two branches will be for the outside of the Peace Sign circle. Bend these two branches into a circle and where they meet, create an approach graft. Bind the graft with the plastic tape.
4 - Complete the Peace Sign by grafting the top of the vertical branch to the top of the circle created by the outside branches.
5 - Prune away any extra shoots that are not part of the design. Allow the branches above the Peace Sign to continue to grow and produce a leaf canopy.

A photograph of this project is located on Page 56.

How to Grow A Chair

There are infinite variations possible in creating a chair design. Here, I present a simple design as a starting point.

Materials needed:

■ 12 tree whips of a pliable nature, such as willow or poplar, each 5' to 6' tall and about 1/2 inch in diameter (bare-root trees are easiest to work with but containerized trees may be used if the soil is washed away. This should only be done when the trees are dormant. Also, prune the roots to allow trees to fit more closely together when planted.)

■ 7 bamboo stakes, each about 3 feet long. Or, use scrap 1 inch wide by 1/4 inch wood stakes.

■ Plastic stretch ties.

■ Baling wire, pliers, wire cutters and a hammer.

■ Optional - 1 stake, about 5 feet long which is used to help train the back of the chair.

1 - Dig a large hole, about two feet by two feet wide and one foot ldeep.

2- Inside the hole, at the location for your chair, mark out the four positions which will serve as the locations for your chair "legs." To ensure a stable finished chair, these "legs" should be about 1 1/2 feet apart and placed in a square pattern. See illustration on next page.

3- Plant four of the tree whips where each front leg is located. This will use up eight of your 12

tree whips.

4 - Where the whips now emerge from the ground, bind the whips tightly. Eight inches above the ground, bind them again. (See figure Page)

5 - Plant two whips at the position for each rear leg. The largest diameter whips should be planted on the outside area of the chair while the

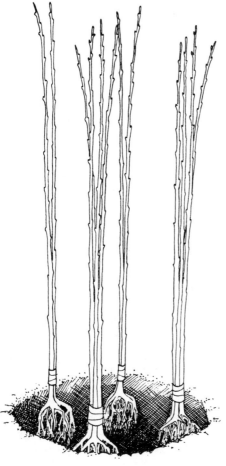

Four bundles of tree whips are planted to become the chair legs. This is the first step in growing a chair.

smaller diameter whips will be to the inside of the chair. These smaller whips will become the chair's arms.

6 - Make a frame for the chair by driving four bamboo stakes into the ground, with each placed to the outside edges of the legs.

7 - To create the front edge of the chair, tie a stake between the front two leg stakes, making it horizontal to the ground This frame should look a bit like a football goal post.

8 - Bend the whips from the front legs over the cross piece of the frame, arching the whips toward the back legs. Starting with the two inside whips, cross these over and under each other to form the chair seat. See illustration at left.

9 - To create the back edge of the chair, a cross piece is

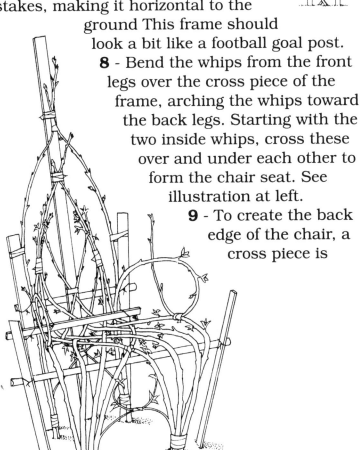

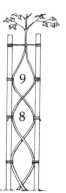

attached to the rear framing stakes using the same method as for the cross piece at the front of the chair. However, the whips from the chair seat are trained UNDERNEATH this cross piece. All the tree whips are now at the rear of the chair, behind this crosspiece.

10 - To bend the whips upward, attach the last stake as a cross piece to the rear leg stakes, about four inches above the lower cross piece. The whips are then threaded IN FRONT of this cross piece, which now forces the whips upward.

11 - Using the inside whips from the bundles of rear leg tree whips, create the chair arms. Bend these whips toward the front of the chair and loop them down to the surface of the chair seat. Where the loop touches the seat, bind it to the whip that is closest to the outside of the chair seat. The remainder of the whip can be woven into the chair seat for extra support. Make sure the

"For me, Trees have always been the most penetrating teachers. I revere them when they live in tribes and families, in forest and groves ... They struggle with all the forces of their lives for one thing only: To fulfill themselves according to their own laws, to build up their own forms, to present themselves. Nothing is holier, nothing is more exemplary, than a beautiful, strong tree."

Hermann Hess

ends of these whips end up higher in the chair than the arm loop.

12 - To achieve an evenly woven pattern in the chair seat, adjust the spacing between the whips. Where whips cross, securely tie the whips together with plastic tie tape.

13 - To finish the chair back, you can pound in the optional stake at the rear of the chair, mid-way between the rear legs. The whips can be woven into a decorative chair back, using the optional stake for extra support.

14 - Finish the chair by using an approach graft to join the whips into a single stem.

15 - Care - During the summer, the whips will produce lots of extra, undesired growth which can be pinched away. Also, refrain from sitting on the chair until it gains enough growth to support weight.

NOTE: Although the instructions call for the whips to be bound with stretch ties, you also can use an approach graft at each point where whips cross. This will form a stronger, more permanent chair structure.

Long Term Care

To finish your sculpture, gather all of your top whips together and graft these into a single trunk. This will prevent competition among the many trees by essentially turning them into a single tree.

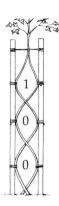

Grafting the tops should be done over a period of time. Begin with just two or three top whips. After these have successfully grafted, add the remaining whips. The idea is that, as you apply these approach grafts, you don't wound any of the whips to the point where a ring of bark has been completely removed from a whip. This would stop the flow of sap to the upper portion of the whip, causing it to die back.

Decide where you want your top graft to be located. At this point remove a strip of bark from five to 10 inches long from each whip, as explained in the section describing approach grafting. Join and bind these whips together with stretch ties.

As the graft forms, a ridge of new tissue will grow between the two whips. Later, one of the two whips can be pruned away, leaving just enough foliage and buds to ensure one more season's growth. After two seasons, the remaining portion of the whip can be pruned away.

Always watch for sprouts along the whip that try to dominate. Pinch these back to ensure the growth of your intended leader. Smaller branches can be left to help protect the main trunks of the trees from sun scald. Keep these side growths short, though, then remove them altogether after a few years.

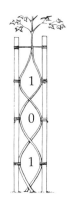

The Maple of Ratibor
attracted crowds in
northern Italy during
the early 1800s.

CHAPTER SIX

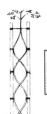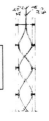

Resources

Books

The Care and Feeding of Trees
Richard Murphy and William Meyer
Crown Publishers 1969

Creative Propagation: A Grower's Guide
Peter Thompson
Timber Press 1993

Gardening by Mail: A Source Book
Barbara J. Barton
Tusker Press 1988

The Grafter's Handbook
R.J. Garner
Oxford University Press 1979

Landscaping with Nature
Jeff Cox
Rodale Press 1991

Living Fences
Ogden Tanner
Chapters Publishing Ltd. 1995

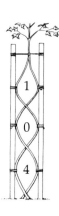 Sunset Western Garden Book
Sunset Books
Lane Publishing Co. 1994

Tayor's Guide to Gardening
Techniques
Houghton Mifflin, 1991

The Complete Book of Topiary
Barbara Gallup and Deborah Reich
Workman Publishing, 1987

Tree Pruning Guidelines
International Society of Arborculture, 1995

100 Tree Myths
Dr. L. Alex Shigo, 1993

Plant Propagation: Principles and Practices
Hudson T. Hartmann, Dale E. Kester and Fred
T. Davies Jr.
Prentice-Hall Inc. 1990

The Complete Book of Pruning
Duncan Coombs,Peter Blackburne-Maze,
Martyn Cracknell, Roger Bentley
Ward Lock, 1994

The Complete Guide to Pruning and Training
Plants
David Joyce and Christopher Brickell
Simon and Schuster, 1992

Shaped Trees and supplies

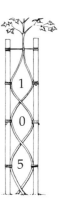

Arborsmith Studios
1067 Caves Camp Road
Williams OR. 97544
(503) 846-7188
After November 1995 (541) 846-7188
Internet address: arborstu@magick.net

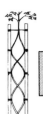
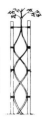

CHAPTER SEVEN

Footnotes

Chapter 1

1 - Lesley Gordon, The Mystery and Magic of Trees and Flowers (Webb & Bower, 1985), P. 9.

2 Rober Graves, The White Goddess, (Peter Smith Pub., Inc., 1983.)

3 Barbara Gallup and Deborah Reich, The Complete Book of Topiary, (Workman Publishing, 1987), P. 16.

4 R.J. Garner, The Grafter's Handbood, (Oxford University Press, 1979), P. 46.

Chapter 4

1 Planetary Planting, Louise Riote, Simon and Schuster, 1975.

2Drope, F., A short and sure guide in the practice of raising and ordering of fruit trees, (Oxford, 1672).

The KEY

Thumb to index
Thumb to middle
Thumb to ring
And thumb to little
Here is the KEY but where is the door?
There's no ceiling and there's no floor.

So I'll turn it while I'm dancing
I'll turn it it while I'm praying
I'll turn it while I'm looking in your eyes
I'll tune it to the stars
I'll tune it to the sun
I'll tune it until we are ONE

Snow